Tennis For Everyone

BY NIKKI SCHULTZ

GROSSET
GOOD LIFE
BOOKS

PUBLISHERS • GROSSET & DUNLAP • NEW YORK

The practice techniques in chapter 3 are patterned after preliminary activities of the EDUCATIONAL RESEARCH COUNCIL OF AMERICA PHYSICAL EDUCATION PROGRAM. Gabriel J. DeSantis and Lester V. Smith. Copyright 1969 by Educational Research Council of America. Published by Charles E. Merrill Publishing Company, Columbus, Ohio.

All photos by Curtis A. Brown,
except where otherwise indicated

Cover photograph by Everett Sherman

Printed in the United States of America

Acknowledgments

Grateful acknowledgment is made to the many tennis players—pro and amateur—who gave so many hours and advice, the United States Lawn Tennis Association for providing some photos and permission to reprint the official tennis rules, and the Educational Research Council of American Physical Education Program for the data used in chapter 3. Special thanks go to the Wilson Sporting Goods Company and *Tennis Illustrated* magazine for many of the photographs appearing in this book, and to Scamp, who assisted in the typing of this manuscript.

Contents

1   All About Tennis   9
2   The Court and Equipment   13
3   Practice Techniques   21
4   Beginning with Basics   33
5   Service   40
6   Basic Strokes   49
7   Specialty Strokes   56
8   Kinds of Play   61
9   Etiquette   68
10 Strategy   72
11 Keeping Score   74
12 A Look at the Pros   76
13 Wrap-Up   84
14 Official Rules   86
    Glossary   93

Tennis For Everyone

1
All About Tennis

ITS PAST

The history of tennis is somewhat of a mystery. It has been traced to ancient Greece, but the closest resemblance to tennis as we know it today began in France and England in the fifteenth or sixteenth century. Some historians say it was played as early as the thirteenth century.

In the beginning, the game was played by hitting a ball (made of fabric and string) with the palm of the hand. The "net" was a rope or a pile of dirt.

The ball was hard and crude, resulting in a lot of sore palms. Some players began to tape their hands, others wore gloves. Later, paddles came into use. No one seems to be certain as to when or how the racket was finally developed.

However, all historians agree that British Major Walter Wingfield deserves the credit for the introduction of modern tennis. It has been said that Major Wingfield used to watch the monks playing a form of court tennis in which a ball was batted against a wall. Wingfield quickly visualized this as a possible fun-type game for his friends.

The ingenious major gave a lawn party in December 1873 and presented his guests with hollow rubber balls and long-handled "rackets." The court was in the shape of an hourglass and was divided by a net. The guests were quickly taught the rules and were delighted with the new game.

The major called the game *sphairistike* (Greek for "to play"), but for obvious reasons the name didn't

Major Walter Wingfield, the inventor of *sphairistike*.

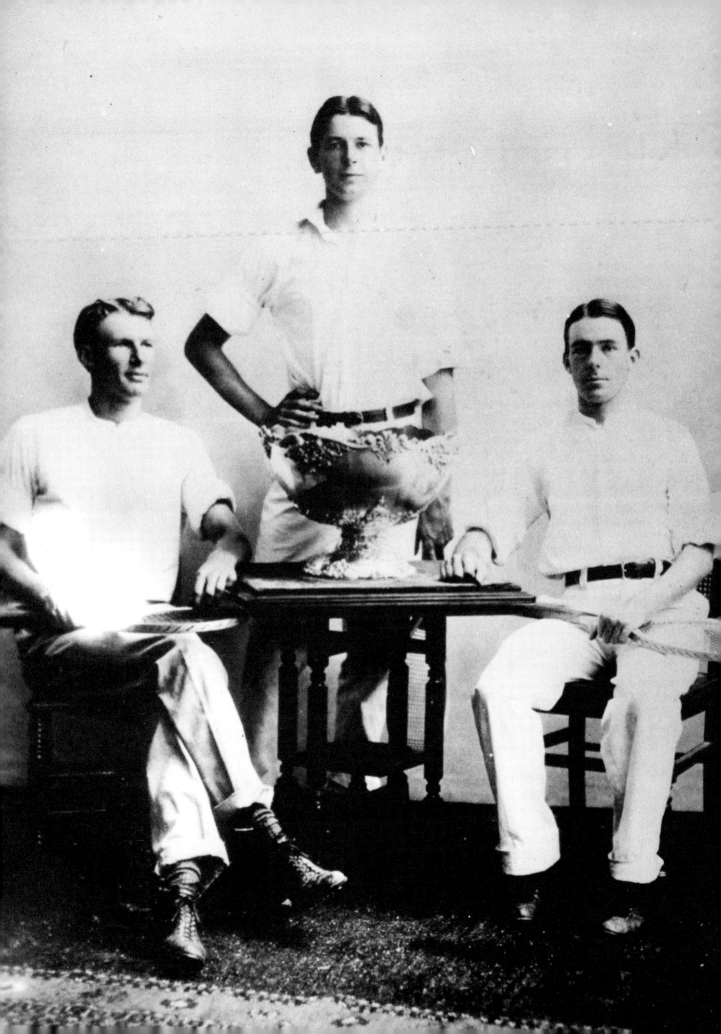

catch on. The *game* did catch on, though, and December 1873 is recorded as the date of the official birth of lawn tennis.

British army officers transferred to posts in Bermuda brought tennis to the Western Hemisphere.

In 1874 a visiting American tourist, Mary Outerbridge, watched the British officers playing a new and unusual game. A sports-minded woman, Miss Outerbridge returned from Bermuda with nets, rackets, and balls. The strange items were quickly confiscated by puzzled customs officers. Eventually, apparently deemed harmless, the items were released and Miss Outerbridge began the happy chore of introducing tennis to America. As women of the day felt the game was not feminine and men felt the game was too feminine, Miss Outerbridge had quite a struggle in the beginning.

Once accepted, the game began to make great strides. In fact, it was so readily received that only a few years later, in 1881, the United States Lawn Tennis Association was formed and rules and equipment became standardized. The United States Lawn Tennis Association is still, to this day, the governing body of tennis in the United States.

Dr. James Dwight, called the father of American tennis, learned to play in 1875 on the second court built in America. He wrote one of the first books about the game and also helped to found the United States Lawn Tennis Association. He was its president from 1891 to 1912.

Dr. Dwight often disputed the claim of Miss Outerbridge, insisting that tennis had come to America from England and that he, rather than she, had played the first tennis in America.

Although history books clearly show that Miss Outerbridge was one year ahead of Dr. Dwight, he deserves much credit for the early promotion and development of the game.

THE DAVIS CUP

An undisputed and very important name in the history of American tennis is that of Dwight Davis. Davis, a varsity-team member at Harvard, was unimpressed with the tennis he saw being played in Britain and suggested inviting a British team to the United States for a match.

Being a man of action, Davis pursued this idea until the British team accepted the challenge. The year was 1900. The elated Davis went out and spent seven hundred dollars on a silver cup to be presented to the winning team.

Davis, himself an outstanding tennis player, was a member of the first Davis Cup team. He won in both singles and doubles play, leading his team in winning his own cup for the glory of America. This was the birth of international team matches and of the highly coveted Davis Cup.

The Davis Cup began as a two-nation tournament, but by the 1970s more than fifty nations were competing.

The competition has been dominated by the United States and Australia, with the United States winning the cup twenty-four times and Australia twenty-three times. Great Britain has won only nine times and hasn't been able to capture the Cup since 1936. France had a six-year winning streak between 1927 and 1932 but hasn't won since.

The only challengers to the United States and Australia in the final rounds were Italy, Mexico, Spain, and India in the 1960s, and West Germany in 1970. Romania started coming on strong in 1969 and was the top challenger to the United States in 1969, 1971, and 1972.

The United States enjoyed a five-year winning streak from 1968 to 1972 but lost to Australia in 1973. Because certain top players were occupied elsewhere during the competition, the United States

The coveted Davis Cup is competed for annually by men's teams of all nations. Since 1937, the United States and Australia have dominated Davis Cup play.

11

lost in the preliminary rounds of 1974 Davis Cup play.

UP TO THE PRESENT

For many years, amateurs competed only against other amateurs, and outstanding players would turn professional. Finally, open competition was accepted, ending the separation between the best players in both the pro and amateur ranks. The change sparked renewed interest in championship competition. In 1968, with the doors opened wide to both pros and amateurs alike, the first Wimbledon Open was taken by pro Rod Laver, while an amateur, Arthur Ashe, won the United States Open.

The excitement generated by open competition stimulated many new players. Tennis began to move. Losing its snob appeal, tennis quickly became a popular sport with whole families taking to the courts.

Increasing financial reward has played its part in promoting and sustaining interest in tennis. In 1974, the World Championship Tennis Tour will offer over one million dollars in prize money to eighty-four male competitors. The United States will have twenty-one players, Australia fourteen. Twenty-four other nations will be represented.

THE GRAND SLAM

Tennis supremacy, not easily gained, is awarded to those players winning a grand slam. This consists of winning four championship tournaments—the Australian, French, United States, and Wimbledon—in one season.

In the history of the game, there have been only four grand slam winners—Don Budge and Maureen Connolly of the United States, and Margaret Smith Court and Rod Laver of Australia. Rod Laver is the only player who has won the grand slam *twice*.

WORLD TEAM TENNIS

Tennis as a spectator sport is being given a try with the advent of World Team Tennis. A total of forty-four matches is played over a three-month season, the first takes place in late spring. Matches are decided by a cumulative scoring of games rather than players winning two straight sets. Some of the players signed with World Team Tennis are Evonne Goolagong, John Newcombe, Rosemary Casals, Jim Connors, and Marita Redondo, with Billie Jean King, Ion Tiriac, Manuel Santana and Tony Roche signed on as player-coaches. Unlike spectator conduct at regular tennis matches, World Team Tennis fans are expected and urged to cheer on their teams.

12

2
The Court
and Equipment

THE COURT

Tennis is played by two players, called singles, or four players, called doubles. The area on which tennis is played is the court and all courts throughout the world are the same size and marked in the same manner.

In a singles game the court is 78 feet long and 27 feet wide and is divided across the middle by a net 3 feet high at the center and 3½ feet at the posts. A singles court has six playing areas: four service courts and two back courts.

In a doubles game the court is 36 feet wide, which increases the playing area but does not affect the service courts.

At the far end of each court is the base line, behind which the server begins play. The service line, which is 21 feet from the net, is 18 feet from and parallel to the base line. Between the service line and the net are the right and left service courts. The 18-foot area between the back line and service line is the back court.

The server must hit the ball into the right or left service court. Each service court is 21 feet by 13½ feet. This puts the ball into play, at which point the only lines that count are the base and sidelines—the ball remains in play as long as it bounces on or within these boundaries. To keep the ball in play, the receiver must return it before it bounces twice.

This sounds simple, but tennis requires quick thinking, fast reflexes, balance, control, stamina, and proper execution of strokes.

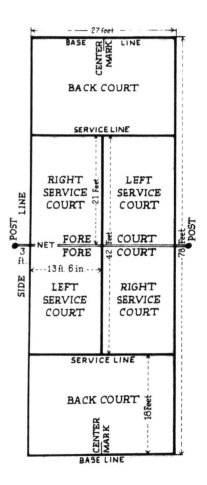

DIAGRAM AND DIMENSIONS
OF SINGLES COURT

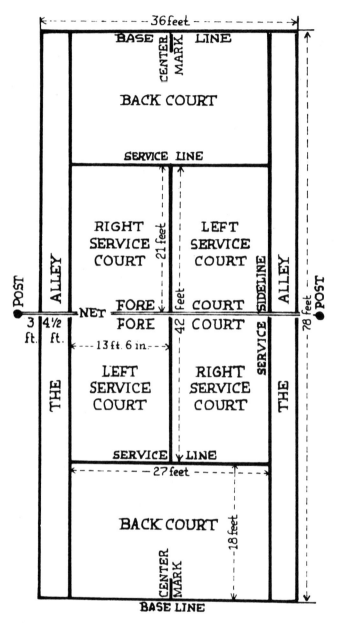

DIAGRAM AND DIMENSIONS
OF DOUBLES COURT

Different types of playing surfaces are used —some are "fast" (the ball bounces hard) and some are "slow" (the ball bounces softly). In order of fastness, the surfaces are: wood, concrete, asphalt, clay, brick, and grass.

Grass courts are used at Wimbledon and for other major tournaments in the eastern part of the United States and in Australia and England. Bounces are easier to control on grass courts than on the hard surfaces of concrete or wood, but maintaining grass courts is expensive; as the popularity of the sport has grown so has the use of the less expensive turfs, such as asphalt. Today, the most widely used surfaces are clay, ground brick, and gravel.

On clay, the ball takes a slow bounce, so the game is usually a slow one with long rallies. Hard serves and volleys lose their effectiveness because of the slower rebound.

The rebound on a concrete court is high and deep. The smoother the surface, the faster the rebound. On concrete courts, aggressive games are played with fast serves and a lot of net play.

Wood is the fastest surface, so players will use very short backswings on the forehand and backhand drives.

THE RACKET

Beginners usually make the mistake of picking too light a racket. Rackets can be light, medium, or heavy. Weight is needed in order to make a good stroke, but a top-heavy racket will cause tiredness in the playing arm and one that's too light will strain arm muscles and cause difficulty in the follow-through.

The proper racket weight is a question of feel and individual preference. Balance of the racket is also important, but is also a matter of personal preference.

Some rackets are heavier in the head, others are heavier in the handle, but it's better to have one more handle-heavy than head-heavy as a top-heavy racket is inclined to swing through too fast on ground strokes and is harder to manipulate.

Contrary to popular belief, rackets are not strung with cat gut but rather nylon, silk, lamb gut, or hog gut. Lamb-gut strings are popular because they offer the most resilience, but they wear very quickly. Nylon seems to be the most suitable for a beginner; it wears well and is less expensive than gut strings. In addition, moisture will destroy gut strings but does not affect nylon.

Tennis rackets come in many styles, weights, and materials.

Rest the center of the racket on your fore and index fingers to test its balance.

Some rackets are made of wood and others of metal. Metal rackets offer less wind resistance and therefore are easier to swing. Metal rackets are also more durable than wood and do not require special attention, such as a racket press.

Completely new to the scene are graphite rackets, which promise the control of wood and the power of metal. They will be on the market in 1974 but will cost $150 and up. Only time will tell if graphite rackets will be an improvement.

Some players have rackets tightly strung, others more loosely. The beginner should have his racket strung between fifty and sixty pounds of tension.

Avoid selecting a racket with a handle (grip) too small for your hand. If a racket turns easily in your hand, try a larger handle. The larger the grip you use, the better.

Your racket is a very important piece of equipment, so take time and care in selecting the one that feels right for you. Don't attempt to make the selection by yourself. Ask the advice of an expert. The salesman at your sporting goods store will guide you with your selection.

THE BALL

A tennis ball is 2½ inches in diameter and weighs two ounces. It is made of hollow rubber covered with a fuzzy white, or the new highly visible yellow, nap. The ball should be replaced as soon as the nap begins to wear off as the flight of the ball becomes inaccurate. Old balls can be used for practicing.

Some tennis balls are sold in attractive pop-top cans. The ring-pull cans are fast and convenient, but should be opened properly and carefully. Don't ignore the directions, or you may receive a scraped or cut finger. Too, never carelessly toss aside the top of the can as it has a razor-sharp edge.

A new pressure-packed can of tennis balls now on the market allows the buyer to open the can, remove and use the balls, then return them to the can, and restore the pressured environment, thereby keeping the stored balls like new longer.

CLOTHING NEEDS

Most public courts have no restrictions on the type or color of clothing worn, but white has always been the traditional choice, although pastels are now acceptable. Many of the women pros now wear two-color ensembles of white dresses trimmed in pastels.

For women, a one-piece tennis dress is the best selection. Shorts or a skirt and blouse are also good choices. In cool weather a lightweight pastel or white cardigan sweater should be used.

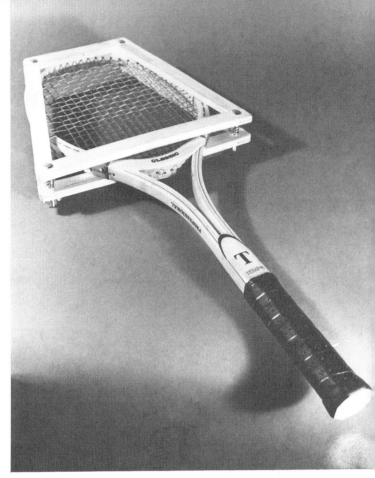

A wooden racket should be kept in a press when not in use.

A metal racket can be kept in a carrying case, ready for a trip to the courts.

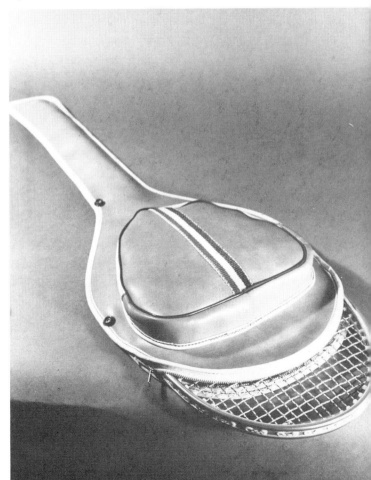

The grip size is usually marked near the handle, as are other markings denoting weight or materials used.

Because the tennis ball is hollow and the rubber rather thin, worn nap easily affects the flight of the ball.

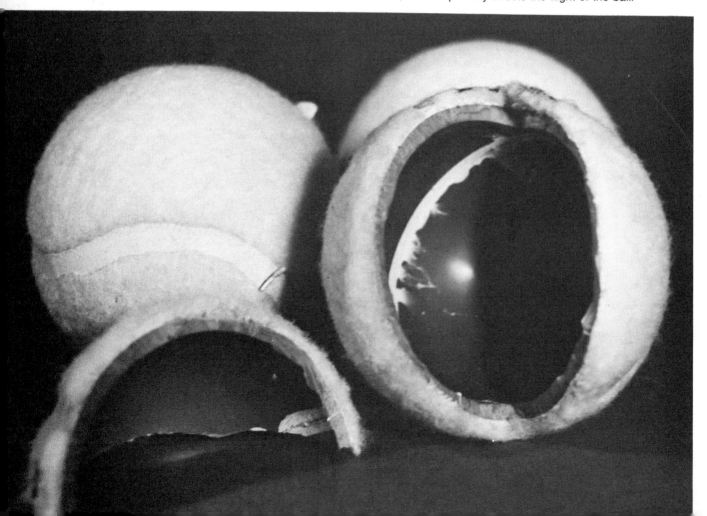

A tennis dress is cool and comfortable, and a matching headband completes the outfit.

For men, shorts or slacks with white T-shirts or polo shirts are proper. Tennis outfits should be loose and comfortable, allowing freedom of movement. Being overly colorful and too casual just doesn't look right.

Keeping your hair neat and in place is important. Tennis visors are practical, as are knitted sweatbands and ribbons. Take a look at the pros and you'll notice that they look cool and neat at all times, even under the most trying circumstances.

Wool or cotton socks are recommended because they are more absorbent than synthetic fabrics. Be certain your socks are free from wrinkles when you play because the friction could cause blistering.

Tennis requires a lot of footwork, so be certain to select shoes that fit properly.

Excess items such as watches and jewelry are not for the court. Avoid sunglasses, if possible, as they can hinder your play. A visor is much more suitable. If you must wear corrective lenses, make sure the glasses are snug enough to prevent slipping or sliding. Elastic glasses-holders are inexpensive and may be helpful during strenuous play.

A sun visor is a handy aid to playing in strong sunlight.

3 Practice Techniques

At first, all that is needed is a ball and a wall target marked 3 or more feet off the ground. Later, a court, partner, and racket can be used in preliminary practice.

TOSS, BOUNCE, AND CATCH

Draw a circle 1 foot in diameter on the floor or ground. Stand facing the circle, one arm length away. Move one side step to the right, so that the circle is diagonally left of your body. Lower your left arm, palm up, to your side. Extend your arm diagonally sideward and upward, tossing the ball high enough to rebound at waist level after it lands in the circle. Swing your right arm toward the ball, catching it in front of your left hip at waist level. Keep practicing the toss, bounce, and catch, gradually increasing the tempo.

WALL THROW AND CATCH

Stand 10 to 20 feet from the wall, with your left foot slightly forward and your left side pointed to the wall target. Throw the ball overhand into the target, then move forward and try to catch the ball on the first bounce at waist level. Practice throwing the ball at various speeds and to different heights to simulate game conditions.

Learn to judge the bounce of the ball and time your movements by wall throw and catch practice, shown in the following five picture sequence.

A

B

C

D

E

READY STANCE, RUN, AND CATCH

Find a partner to throw the ball from the other side of the net. Face your partner with your hands on your knees, feet spread to about shoulder width, with weight on the balls of your feet. Keep your eyes on your partner. He should throw the ball to your right or left. Try to catch the ball on the first bounce, throw it back to your partner, and immediately return to your ready stance. Ask your partner to throw the ball at different speeds.

Later, ask your partner to throw the ball to you as you try to meet it on the first bounce and hit it back over the net with a racket.

Practice footwork and timing by reacting, from your ready stance, to your partner's throw.

Once you have coordinated timing and footwork, try to "meet" the ball with the racket.

A racket cover makes a handy kneeling pad.

BALL TAPPING TO GROUND

With palm down, hold your racket by the throat with racket face parallel to ground. Kneel on the ground (or on a handy racket cover) and hit the ball consecutively twenty-five to one hundred times. Repeat this ball-tapping exercise while standing. Continue to practice this exercise from kneeling and standing positions, then practice the same exercise while moving around.

BALL TAPPING UPWARD

With palm up, grasp the racket by the throat with racket face parallel to ground. While standing, hit the ball upward 6 to 8 inches, twenty-five to one hundred times in succession.

Bounce the ball while in a stationary standing position, then practice the same exercise while moving around.

Keeping the ball in the air for one hundred bounces demands concentration and coordination.

READY STANCE

Your ready stance can be practiced by facing the net squarely with feet spread comfortably apart, weight on the balls of your feet, knees bent, body relaxed and slightly crouched. Cradle the racket in front of your body at thigh level, racket parallel to ground, face flat and pointed directly ahead. Your left hand should be at the throat of the racket, with your right hand on the grip. Continue to practice cradling the racket until it feels comfortable. Flex your knees and bounce without lifting your feet to get a feeling of proper balance.

It is important to be able to assume the proper ready stance quickly and feel "at home" in it.

From ready stance, practice pivoting . . .

PIVOTING

Pivoting can be practiced in a real or imaginary circle. Assume your ready stance with your racket pointing to 12 o'clock. Directly behind you is 6 o'clock, to your right is 3 o'clock and to your left, 9 o'clock. Rotate your hips to the right, pivoting on the soles of both feet until your toes are pointed to 3 o'clock. Keep the racket parallel to the floor. Rotate back to ready stance at 12 o'clock. Now rotate your hips to the left, pivoting on the soles of your feet until your toes are pointed to 9 o'clock.

Continue practicing the pivot to the right and left. Your arm should be relaxed and slightly bent. Keep the racket in proper position for a beginning stroke; for example, when your toes are pointed to 3 o'clock in a right pivot, the racket head should be at 2 o'clock and moving clockwise. When your toes are pointed to 9 o'clock in a left pivot, your racket head is at 10 o'clock and moving counterclockwise.

to the right (3 o'clock) . . .   back to center . . .

31

. . . then pivot to the left (9 o'clock).

4
Beginning with Basics

GRIP

The most widely used grip is the Eastern, the advantage being that the grip is comfortable, can be switched from forehand to backhand, and is convenient for high and low strokes. The Eastern grip is made by "shaking hands" with the racket.

Variations of this grip are the Continental and Western grips. With the Continental grip, you place the racket on its edge and then pick it up. With the Western grip you lay the racket flat on the ground and pick it up. You should find the grip most comfortable for you.

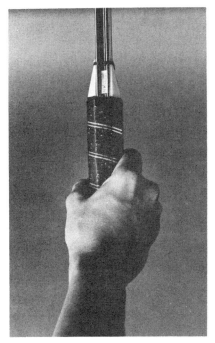

Eastern grip

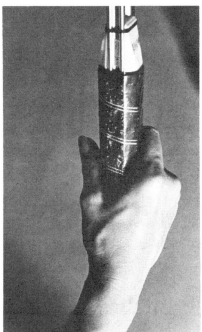

Continental grip

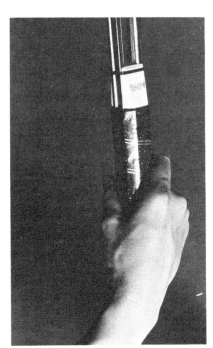

Western grip

Notice that the "V" formed by the joining of the thumb and the index finger falls to the left of the center of the handle for the Eastern grip; at the center in the Continental grip; and to the right in the Western grip.

Here is a front view of the Continental grip.

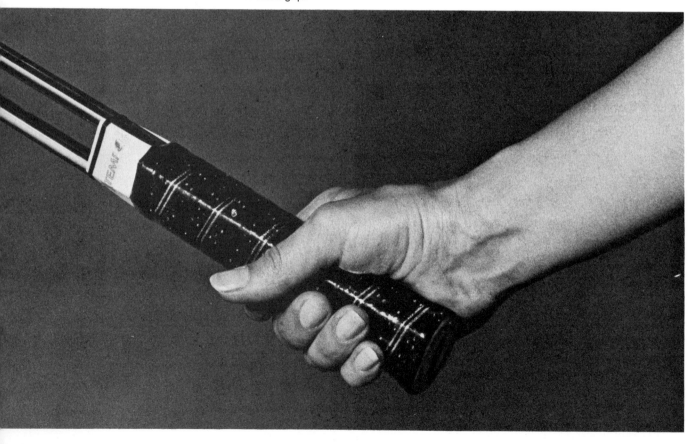

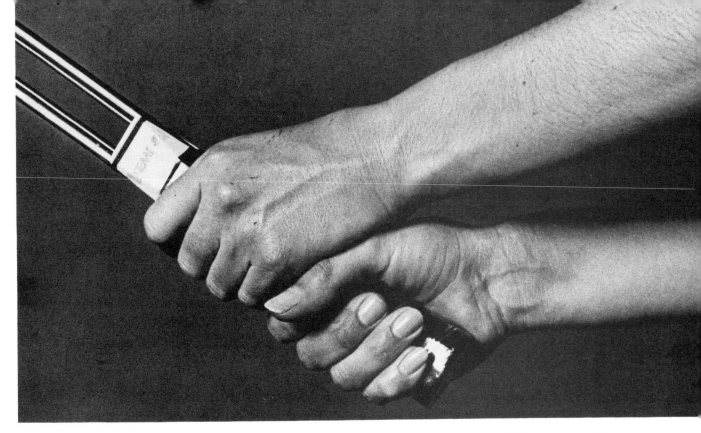

Forehand and backhand views of the two-handed grip. The lower hand is the grip hand, the upper one adds extra strength.

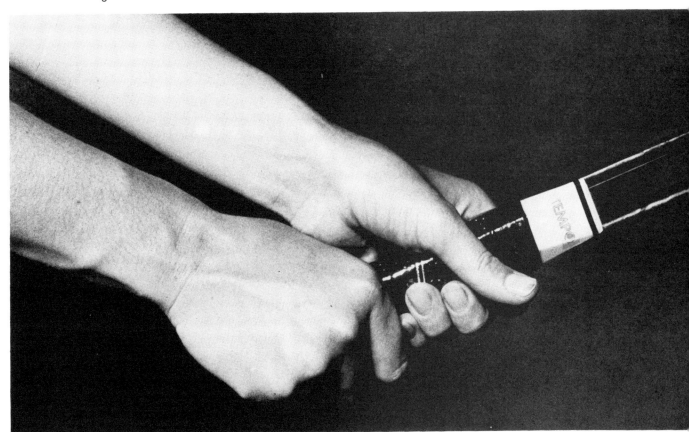

If your opponent consistently hits to your forehand, use the forehand grip. If the ball comes to your backhand, you can make a quick switch.

Attempt a grip midway between the backhand and forehand; that way only a small adjustment will be needed. A midway grip is a good rule of thumb; if you hold an extreme forehand grip, your backhand grip might be weak and vice versa.

A two-handed grip will give you a strong swing but it also shortens reach, which is why so few players use it with any degree of success. It isn't recommended that this grip be adopted, but try it once in a while. Some players find great success with the unorthodox. Do not hesitate to experiment.

READY STANCE

A ready position is very important as it will increase your chances of a good return. You should return to a ready stance as soon as possible after every stroke.

Good balance is important as it will enable you to move quickly in any direction. Your feet should be about 12 to 18 inches apart, with your body weight on the balls of your feet.

Keep a firm grip on the racket, but don't "choke" it. Cradle the racket in your left hand and flex your knees so that your body bends forward slightly. Keep your eyes on the ball. If it is coming to your right, push off with your left foot. If it is coming to your left, push off with your right foot.

Without the ready stance a player is not ready for action, so the ready stance is not a passive pose but an active motion showing your opponent that you are ready.

To recap, here is a six-point program to a proper ready stance:

1. Face the net with legs comfortably apart.
2. Bend knees slightly.
3. Body should be slightly forward with weight evenly distributed on balls of feet.
4. Point tip of racket toward net, with head of the racket slightly higher than waist level.
5. Balance racket by gripping firmly and cradling the "throat" in your left hand.
6. Keep your eyes on the ball at all times.

Tennis pro Chris Evert uses the two-handed grip very effectively.

With his eye on the ball and in ready stance, tennis great Jack Kramer signals that he is ready for action.

Six points to a proper ready stance.

Rod Laver's left-handedness didn't stop him from defeating right-handers Roy Emerson in 1962 and Tony Roche in 1969 for two National Men's Singles Championships.

LEFT-HANDED?

The guidelines in this book are for right-handed players, but a left-hander need only reverse the instructions. Left-handers should not attempt to play right-handed.

If you are left-handed, learn to serve and play in the left court, which will enable you to play more forehands. Your backhand might tend to be weak and might become a burden when playing against a strong opponent. With careful practice and control you might be able to overcome this handicap. There are many fine left-handed players—Rod Laver is a good example, as is the up-and-coming Manuel Orantes of Spain.

If possible, take lessons from a coach who can guide you. Don't be inhibited. Remember, left-handers are built no differently from right-handers. Anyone who has been demolished by Laver or Orantes will readily attest to that.

One important point to keep in mind is that you, as a left-hander, are one step ahead in the strategy of the game. You will find that players facing a left-hander are inclined to change their game. They do not feel comfortable serving and hitting to what would normally be the strong forehand of a right-hander. Too, an opponent must keep your "handicap" in mind throughout the game and place the ball accordingly, or risk being caught off balance. Use this to your advantage.

5
Service

Learn to take advantage of this stroke; a good service will immediately put your opponent on the defensive. Be patient, though, as service takes time to master.

A fast and hard service will give your opponent less time to react, so sacrifice accuracy and a possible fault on your first serve. You've got a second serve, if necessary, which you can hit with more control and less force. For the first serve, aim right for your opponent rather than to his right or left. In order to make a return, he'll have to move out of the way of your serve rather than simply turning right or left to make his return. If you place a service well and hit it so hard that it cannot be returned, it is called a *service ace*.

If your serve hits the top of the net yet lands in the proper service court, it does not count and is called a *let*. You'll have to make the serve over. If you serve before your receiver is ready (in his ready stance), it is also called a *let*.

Ideally your first serve should be made hard and fast, and aimed directly at your opponent.

If the ball does not fall into the proper service court, it is called a *fault* and a second serve is allowed. If the second serve is not proper it is called a *double fault*, and a point is awarded your opponent.

When serving, you play the first point from the right of the center mark and serve the ball diagonally across the court to your left into the opponent's right service court. The receiver must wait for the ball to bounce and is not allowed to return it on the fly. The next point is served from the left of the center mark into your opponent's left service court and then alternately behind your right and left courts until the game is finished.

You have two tries to make a legal serve. If the first serve is good, the ball is in play. If the first serve is not good, serve again. If the second serve is not good, you lose the point. Your foot is not allowed to touch the line or step into the court until after the ball has been served, or you are charged with a *foot fault*.

Be sure your foot is *behind* the service line as you get into position to serve.

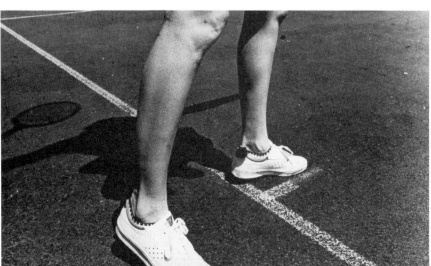

Stepping into the court before the ball has been hit is a foot fault.

41

GRIP

The grip used is a matter of personal preference. For beginners, the regular forehand grip is recommended. Later, the Continental grip (used by most pros) can be tried. In the Continental grip, the fingers are spread out more than in the forehand grip and the forefinger extends up the handle, allowing more flexibility of the wrist.

STANCE

Stand a few inches behind the base line with your left foot at a 45-degree angle to it, and your toes pointing toward the right. Your right foot should be parallel to the base line and, for proper balance, about 12 to 18 inches behind the left foot. Your weight should be on your back foot, and your left shoulder pointed to the court where the ball is to be served. Hold the racket toward the net with your wrist approximately chest level and the racket head about level with your face. Your body should be relaxed and your stance comfortable.

Hold the two balls and the racket toward the net at about eye level in preparation for the toss.

Release the first ball a little above shoulder level.

Practice both placing the ball and the service sequence, tossing the ball so that it will bounce in the racket cover after "meeting"—not hitting—it with the racket.

THE TOSS

It is customary to hold two balls so that the second is ready for use should the first service be a fault or a let. The first ball is held between the first two fingers and the thumb. The second is held by the ring and little finger in the lower, fleshy part of the thumb. Some players can hold three balls, but this isn't necessary or recommended for beginners.

The first ball is released by opening the first two fingers and thumb when the arm is a little above shoulder level. Until you have learned to master the timing, it's best to toss the ball high so that you will have time to hit it as it falls. If you toss it too low, you might hit it with the edge of your racket or miss it completely.

You must learn to toss the ball at the same speed and to the same place every time. Ideally, the ball should be hit at the top of the toss. Reach up with your racket outstretched to measure the proper height of your toss. A poor serve can usually be traced to a faulty tossing technique. If you can master and perfect the toss, the rest of your service will be reasonably simple.

Remember, if you aren't satisfied with your toss you don't have to hit it—you can catch the ball and toss again.

THE SWING AND HIT

When tossing the ball, simultaneously start your backswing. Bring the racket back in a relaxed, backward-to-upward circular motion and then up overhead. Your elbow will bend, bringing the racket behind your shoulders and head at the back of your neck. From this cocked position, shift your body weight to your left foot. The wrist and elbow are then snapped upward into a fully extended position overhead. Stand on your toes and reach for the ball. As the racket hits the ball, snap your wrist forward. Follow through with the racket to the left side of your body, near your ankle. Return to ready stance. Do not follow your service into the net.

TYPES OF SERVICE

There are three types of service: slice, the American twist, and the flat service. Grip, stance, and delivery for all three serves are basically the same. How the racket strikes the ball and the follow-through determine the type of stroke.

The Slice: This is the easiest serve to learn and control, and is recommended for beginners because it takes little effort. In a slice service, the racket is rotated slightly during the swing, causing the racket to cut across, hitting the ball with a glancing blow.

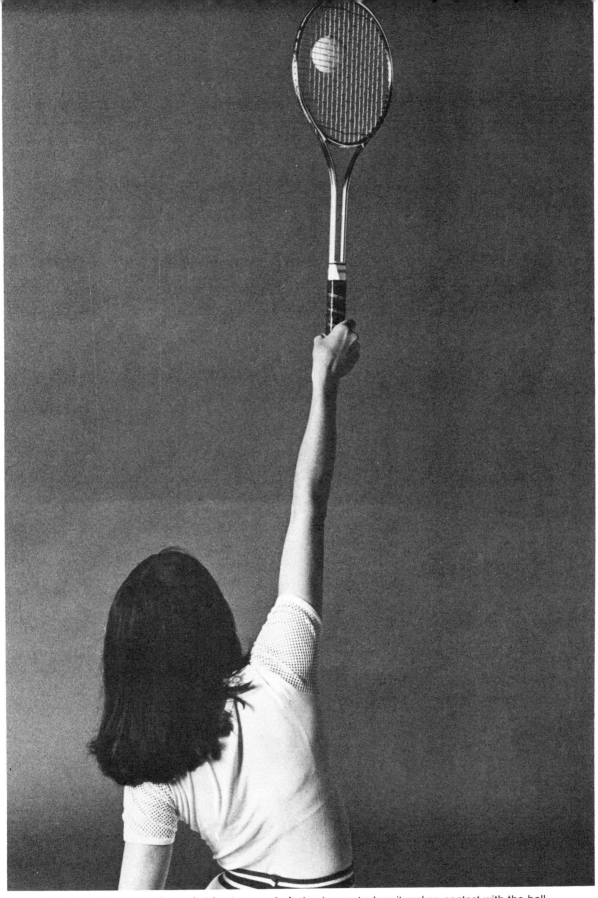

For the slice serve, the racket is at an angle facing in-court when it makes contact with the ball.

The demanding American twist service necessitates turning the face of the racket slightly outward and making contact with the ball with the racket moving upward rather than forward.

The slice causes the ball to spin sideways and curve downward when it leaves the racket. The downward curve, hopefully, will be to the left and away from your opponent's forehand. If you are the receiver of a slice serve, try to return it with your forehand. If your opponent makes a toss to his right, you can safely assume that you will be receiving a slice serve.

The American Twist: A physically demanding service, the American twist is not recommended for beginners. It is the most difficult serve to learn. The grip used is the same as for the backhand stroke. The toss is made slightly back and to the left. Impact occurs directly above the back. The ball is struck with an upward motion, causing it to spin in flight and to take a high bounce when it hits the ground. This is a difficult serve to return, so be prepared if you see your opponent making the toss to his left. If the serve is to your backhand, try to block it with a high backhand stroke. If the serve is to your forehand, try to hit over the ball, using a top spin. If your racket is too low and you swing down on the ball, you'll probably hit the net.

The Flat or Cannonball: As its name implies, the flat (or cannonball) serve is a hard hit service, resulting in little or no spin on the ball. The ball blazes into the opponent's court in an almost straight line. The difference between the slice and flat serve is that in the flat serve the wrist is given only a slight turn. The ball is hit directly on top with the racket face flat. This serve can be risky for players of below-average height as the ball must clear the net by only a few inches or it will come down out of the court. If you see this quick serve coming your way, remember that it will bounce to about waist level, so use a short backswing with a full follow-through to return the serve.

PRACTICING YOUR SERVE

Beginners should concentrate on the slice serve before trying the flat or American twist serves. Practice your service stroke by hitting the ball against a wall approximately 30 feet away. Practice the rhythm of your service without a ball, as your feet and legs play an important function in the fluid movement necessary for a proper service. To get the correct rhythm, say and do: "backswing, cock arm, shift weight, hit, follow through." The toss of the ball should be simultaneous with your backswing.

When the ball is hit hard with the racket face flat (parallel to the net), it will cannonball over the net.

6
Basic Strokes

There are three fundamental tennis strokes: the serve, which we have already discussed; the drive (forehand and backhand); and the volley (forehand and backhand).

DRIVE

The drive is a ground stroke; that is, it is used to return the ball after it has bounced once. Most points are won with the forehand drive, so after the service, this is the most important stroke to learn.

Forehand Drive: Thankfully, in addition to being one of the most important strokes, the forehand drive is the easiest stroke to learn.

If you watch a pro game you'll see many forehand drives played with naturalness and confidence. The pro turns easily into a sideways-to-the-net position, meets the ball at waist level, and hits it firmly and smoothly across the net. It appears to be one complete, natural, fluid motion. This is what you must attempt to do.

Use the grip that feels most natural to you. Cradle the throat of the racket in your left hand, pointing the racket head toward the net. Assume ready stance.

Start your backswing early, if possible, as soon as your opponent hits the ball. Don't wait until you reach the ball.

As the ball is hit to your forehand, take a sideways-to-the-net position and backswing for a forehand drive.

Be alert to the orientation of the racket as it makes contact with the ball for a split-second more reaction time.

For the forehand drive, shift your weight to your front foot before meeting the ball.

As you begin your backswing, your wrist should "break" in front of your body, bringing the racket to the right. Continue to move the arm in a backward sweep. By the time your racket reaches your hip, you should begin to pivot and the forward swing will begin as the ball approaches, shifting your weight back to your front foot. As you meet the ball, the racket should hit through it, with the elbow extending forward in the direction of the hit.

The follow-through finds the racket continuing in an upward direction. After the point of impact, follow through by leaning your weight into the ball, finishing with the racket head coming to a stop opposite your left shoulder.

Recapping the forehand drive: when the ball comes to you, pivot to the side on which the ball will bounce. For example, if the ball is coming toward you on the right, pivot with your right foot and cross over with your left foot, which will bring your feet parallel to the net and pointing to the right sideline. Your left shoulder will be pointing toward the net. Shift your weight to your right foot and, at the same time, swing the racket back as far as possible and attempt to have the backswing lined up with the approaching ball. Keep the head of the racket slightly below the anticipated height following the bounce of the ball. Shift your weight from your back foot to your front foot. Get a firm grip on the racket and try to hit the ball with the center of your racket. Do *not* crowd the ball or your elbow will bend too

Continue the forehand drive stroke to a full follow-through.

much, disrupting the clean forehand stroke.

Remember, there are four distinct phases: back-swing, forward swing, contact, and follow-through. Your rhythm should be developed enough for your stroke to be continuous and smooth. This, of course, means that practice is essential.

Backhand Drive: A backhand drive is used when the ball has bounced to the left of a right-handed player or to the right of a left-handed player. This stroke will feel awkward at first, but with patience and practice it can be easily mastered.

As in the forehand, the backhand should be one continuous, smooth motion.

The backswing begins from your ready position. If you see the ball coming to your left side (assuming that you are right-handed) rotate the racket to the left for the backhand grip. The racket will still be cradled in your left hand, so use your left hand to pull the racket back about waist high until your left hand is resting near the left hip. Rotate your shoulders and hips so that you end up sideways to the net with your weight on your back foot.

As the ball approaches, begin your forward swing, rotating hips and shoulders forward along with the racket. Your weight will gradually shift to your front foot. Bend your knee and lean your shoulder into the ball.

The ball should be hit from 6 to 10 inches in front of the forward foot and to the left of your body. Your grip should be firm, with your elbow slightly bent.

51

In a backhand sideways-to-the-net position, practice coordinating the forward swing and follow-through with the gradual shifting of weight to your front foot.

After you hit the ball, straighten your elbow, guiding it in the direction of the hit. Continue to extend your arm and racket forward and upward until your racket is about shoulder high. Your shoulders and hips will have rotated along with your follow-through and you will find yourself again facing the net and in position to resume your ready stance.

Proper stance and the backswing are coordinated more closely in a backhand drive than in forehand. If you see the ball coming to your backhand, pivot, turning your shoulder toward the net and keeping the weight of your body on the back foot. The racket will be behind you and can be at hip level or approximately shoulder height. Gradually transfer the weight of your body as the ball approaches and attempt to hit the ball at waist level.

Your first attempt at hitting backhand will probably send the ball into the net. Do not be discouraged. The same thing undoubtedly happened to Billie Jean King and Stan Smith.

To get backhands over the net you must meet the ball farther ahead of your hip than in forehands. Hit the ball straight and use a long contact.

VOLLEY

A volley is the stroke used to hit the ball before it touches the ground. Volleys are often confused with rallies, which are another prolonged series of strokes but consist of ground strokes as well as volleys. A volley, forehand or backhand, is used mainly when you are playing the net, although volleys can be made from almost any part of the court.

Volleys are used when playing aggressive doubles games and in singles games when you are forced to rush the net to hit short returns. Pivoting and long follow-through are eliminated.

In a volley, you should step toward the ball and "punch" it back to your opponent. There is no backswing as in a ground stroke. Do not bend forward. Keep your back straight and bend only from the knees. On low shots, your knees might come close to touching the ground, but remember not to move your weight forward.

On a high volley, punch in a downward direction, with the face of the racket almost flat or perpendicular to the ground. On low volleys, tilt the racket face back a little; this will enable your return to easily clear the net. The lower the volley, the more the racket should be tilted skyward.

Use the same grips for forehand and backhand volleys as you do for forehand and backhand drives. If you have not yet mastered the switch from forehand grip to backhand grip, use a grip midway between the two or try to use the Continental grip, which can be used for either type of shot. In the beginning, choke up on the racket handle. When you've gained some confidence and experience, switch to the grip best suited for your style of play.

Forehand Volley: For a forehand volley, assume the ready stance in the middle of the court about 6 to 8 feet from the net. Crouch a little deeper than usual as this will enable you to keep a better eye on the

A racket angled according to the height of the oncoming ball will allow the volley to clear the net.

To give the ball its proper "punch," your weight should be on your left foot in a forehand volley. Fast footwork takes alertness and practice.

ball. You'll also be able to move faster to the right or left. The racket should be tilted away and held upward in front of your chest instead of parallel to the ground. Hit the ball well in front of your body. Your hand will be laid back, palm parallel to the net. Hit behind and down on the ball, which will give it backspin. Stop the racket at the point of impact. Quickly return to ready stance with racket high.

Backhand Volley: If you are at the net and the ball comes to your left, you should use a backhand volley. Again, you should crouch a little deeper than you would for a backhand drive. If you see that the return can be played as a backhand volley, move your right foot up so that the placement is about the same as for the backhand drive, with the weight of your body on the back foot, rear knee bent, and right knee "sagged." For added firmness, use both hands on the racket when striking the ball. If possible, turn

sideways to the net. The racket face should be tilted slightly to give the ball some backspin.

Fast footwork is required when volleying, so stay alert and keep your eyes on the ball at all times. You must meet the ball with the center of your racket. Don't reach out for the ball; it should be hit with the weight of your body behind it. Never pause or linger—if the ball is coming too fast, simply throw your weight on the foot nearest the ball (left foot for forehand, right foot for backhand), pivot, do not turn, and *never* step backward in a volley shot.

Without a ball, practice your stroke and footwork. Practice keeping your wrist locked, knees bent, and weight distributed properly. Take turns throwing and volleying with a partner. Your partner should throw the ball overhand, while you practice hitting the ball downward across the tape of the net. Start slowly and increase the pace.

7
Specialty Strokes

To learn a well-rounded game of tennis it is necessary to know all of the basic strokes (service, drive, volley), plus the lob, smash, chop or dink, drop shot, slice, half-volley, and so forth.

LOB

This is a soft ground stroke in which the ball is lifted high in the air. The lob is usually executed as a defensive measure but if it is made unexpectedly it can be a smart, point-winning play.

An offensive lob, if correctly disguised, can catch an opponent off balance. If you are inside the base line and your opponent is crowding the net, an offensive lob, just high enough to clear your opponent's outstretched racket, will either win a point for you or force your opponent away from the net. If your opponent has to run back, rush the net yourself and get into volleying position.

If you receive an offensive lob, try to return it with a smash (explained on this page). If the lob is low and you can't get it into the air, let it bounce and try to retaliate with a defensive lob.

The defensive lob can be used when you need a better position or when you are undecided as to what stroke to use. Your return should be sky high and deep into the court so that you will have time to get back on equal terms with your opponent. Keep in mind that an overhead smash is one answer to a lob, so if your opponent has sight of the ball, don't rush the net on a defensive lob. Stay behind the base line so that you can return the smash he'll undoubtedly be using.

Do not try to return a defensive lob until the ball bounces. The high-lobbed ball will be traveling straight down at you and accelerating, so you might possibly mistime the stroke, or even miss the ball completely.

Lobs can be made either forehand or backhand. In the forehand, use the forehand grip, bringing the racket in a low forehand backswing, upper body forward. Hit *under* the ball, below waist level, following through with the racket pointed at the ball in flight. Try for height, not distance.

In the backhand lob, use the backhand grip and a low backhand backswing, knees bent, weight on the back (left) foot. Shift your weight to the front (right) foot, hitting *under* the ball below waist level, with the same follow-through as with the forehand lob.

Most lobbing is done on the run, so fast footwork and practice are essential.

SMASH OR OVERHEAD

The smash or overhead shot is a hard overhead swing on a descending ball and is the answer to your opponent's lob. To execute a smash, use a forehand grip and the ready stance used for a forehand volley, with racket held high. Step backward, left side to the net, feet parallel and wide apart. Bring your racket above and to the right of your head with your right hand and hit the ball, snapping your wrist forward above and in front of your right shoulder. You might have to stretch or jump to make this stroke, using a scissors kick of the legs. After impact, face the net and let the racket go through to a full follow-through.

If you are on the receiving end of an overhead

With your weight shifted to the right foot for a backhand lob, hit *under* the ball and follow through.

A defensive lob, lofting high into the air and sailing deep, gives you time to get back into good court position.

To be in position for the smash, the lobbed ball should be coming right at you. A deep lob makes it necessary to back up to get into position.

A scissor kick may help you to reach a high ball and add power to your stroke, but control is diminished in losing contact with the ground.

smash, turn sideways, keep your eye on the ball, and retreat, if possible without crossing your feet to keep your weight properly balanced. If in doubt about the speed of the ball, remember that it is better to retreat too far back and then have to take a step or two forward than not to go back far enough and have the ball get by you before you are ready to hit it. Try to return the smash as though you are serving—hit it hard and aim for the center of the court.

Timing the return of a lob is important, so practice is essential. Ask a partner to toss balls in the air to you. Start about 10 feet from the net and gradually increase the distance as you continue to practice the smash. Then you and your partner can take turns hitting lobs and returning them with smash shots.

CHOP SHOT

This defensive stroke is primarily used to change the pace of the game. The racket is drawn down sharply with a chopping motion, forcing the ball into a backspin or underspin.

The deep chop (underspin) is effective against the American twist service or on high-bounding balls. The soft chop (also called a *dink*) is used when you are playing the net and your opponent is playing

After hitting the ball, continue the stroke to a full follow-through.

When your opponent is in the back court, a soft chop over the net can earn you a fast point.

deep. Chop shots can be made forehand or backhand.

DROP SHOT

This is a ground stroke in which the ball just barely clears the net. It is a difficult shot, hit with an underspin. A forehand or backhand drive can be used. A drop shot is used only from inside the service line and only when your opponent is very deep or far out of position. The ball is played on a bounce and resembles a minilob, only with a backspin. A drop shot is used for a change of pace or to catch an opponent off balance. But don't attempt this shot until you have become a seasoned player, for if you bounce the ball too high, you will give your opponent a sure point.

DROP OR STOP VOLLEY

This stroke is similar to the drop shot, except that the ball is hit *before* it bounces. In order to make this shot you must be only a few feet from the net, as it is used only when your opponent is on the base line, moving in the wrong direction or out of position. In a drop volley, come up sharply under the ball, pulling the arm back just at impact and turning the wrist under.

59

The pick-up shot is used when a player is on his way to the net and refuses to retreat.

HALF-VOLLEY

Also called a Pick-Up Shot, this isn't a volley but rather a ground stroke since the ball does bounce. The short-backswing stroke is used to return balls that have bounced at a player's feet. It is important to get down behind the ball, and to adjust the amount of follow-through according to your distance from the net. For a half-volley from mid-court, keep the follow-through short.

Beginners should step back in order to avoid the extremely hard to handle half-volleys—even advanced players tend to avoid hitting this shot.

60

8
Kinds of Play

SINGLES

In singles play, there is a player on each side of the net. If you win the coin toss (or racket spin), choose to serve.

Play begins when the server, standing behind his base line and to the right of the center mark, tosses the ball in the air and serves it over the net into the diagonally opposite service court or upon any line bounding it. Try to serve directly to your opponent or to his backhand rather than his forehand.

After the ball has bounced on the ground, the receiver must return the ball over the net to the playing area bounded by the sidelines and base line. Attempt to clear the net by 10 or 12 feet and try to make as few errors as possible.

In the beginning, concentrate on footwork, ready stance, basic strokes, and keeping your eye on the ball. Don't try to hit the ball hard. Try to keep a rally going for as long as possible.

Play continues with the ball being hit in the air before bouncing on the ground (volley) or on the first bounce (ground stroke), thus going back and forth over the net (rallying) until one player misses. The object is to win the point by making your opponent miss. You can do this by driving the ball past him, placing it where he is unable to return it before it bounces twice, or causing him to hit the ball so that it comes down outside the court boundaries or slams into the net.

Your first singles sets should be played from the base line, where the slower place will be easier for you. Try for depth, which will force your opponent

For the beginner, the return-of-serve calls for a full stroke lifting the ball high over the net so that it lands deep in his opponent's court.

To start, don't hit the ball hard. The longer the rally, the more chance you have to practice your strokes.

Once you are comfortable with the slower pace of ground-stroke play at the base line, advance to the net and try to work in a few volleys.

to hit the ball from the back of his court and give you more time to get into position to return the shot.

Later, as you gain confidence, start playing an all-court game—advance to the net if you see a chance to volley your opponent's shot. This will force your opponent to change his game if he has gotten into the habit of making deep drives.

You'll learn that a point is easier to win from net play than from base-line play, but don't use a close-to-the-net position as the pros do. Their reflexes are faster than yours. Right now, your net game should be at least 3 yards from the net.

Don't force your developing abilities. Patience is important.

DOUBLES

A whole new approach is required in doubles play—the court is larger, there are more players, and most of the scoring is usually from the net position. Naturally, teamwork is absolutely essential.

If possible, find a partner who excels where you are weak. Then plan your method of attack. If you have not developed hand signals with your partner, it's important to talk during play, calling out "yours" or "mine" or "I've got it."

Doubles partners should try to maintain a side-by-side position, thereby giving each player a narrow area to cover. In doubles, a net position midway between the net and the service line is the most solid defensive maneuver. If one player is at the net and the other is deep, your opponents can use a cross-court placement for points, so a parallel line of defense is important. In watching matches you'll note that pros play almost toe-to-toe doubles, and net play is the key to success.

For net play, the Continental grip is recommended, but you should experiment with grips in order to find the proper balance. Grip the racket and hold it at a 90-degree angle in front of you, with the tip under your chin and the other hand at the throat of the racket. Always maintain a ready stance.

If the ball comes to you, use a stroke shorter than a ground stroke and punch at the ball, using very little backswing. Hit down on the ball if possible and try to aim for your opponent's feet. When in doubt, try to hit the ball between your two opponents.

If you must hit up, use a lob, the most underrated shot in doubles. Make it high and deep to get your opponents away from the net. A light touch is essential in doubles play. The strategy is to avoid a slashing attack—how and where you place the ball is more important.

The side-by-side doubles position gives each player the narrowest area to cover.

Unlike a singles game, the server is at a disadvantage in doubles. Following your serve, it is important to advance to the net quickly and attempt to capture it.

A ball down the middle could cause confusion if players aren't used to doubles. Ideally the player nearest the ball should reach it with a forehand stroke; his partner backing up the play.

On the return of serve, your best volley is a soft one, keeping the ball low and forcing your opponent to hit up. Hit your volley hard and deep only if your opponent has not approached the net after his return.

In serving, a slice will enable you to immediately reach the net. Using volleys and smash shots will keep you at the net. The server, usually at an advantage in a singles game, is at a disadvantage in a doubles game because his partner must drop back, permitting the opponents to capture the net. Immediately after your serve, run toward the net to join your partner, who should be about 6 feet from the net, facing the receivers, and advance together.

Return of service is important, so take a few chances in order to gain time and net position.

The general rule is that each partner should play the balls coming to his side of the court. When a ball is hit down the middle, it should be returned by the player who can reach it first with a forehand. If you and your partner are playing the net and the ball is lobbed over your partner's head, it is easier for you to run back and play the ball, and vice versa.

Remember, the team capturing the net and holding that position will win the point.

9 Etiquette

Many of the customs of the game are not included in the official rules (reprinted in full on pages 86–91), and while you don't need to know all the rules in fine detail to enjoy the game, you should learn the basic rules and the unwritten rules of good sportsmanship. This is the first step to achieving the fullest pleasure from the game. In addition, you'll speed up and improve your game in the process.

ATTITUDE

A good sportsman will be enthusiastic and interested even when playing with an opponent who does not play in his class. Acting bored or disinterested is a poor attitude. Try to make the game fun and interesting for everyone.

You should learn to praise good shots (without overdoing it). If your partner doesn't play at your level, slow down and concentrate on keeping the ball in play. Use this time for perfecting the fundamentals and practicing the specialty strokes. Don't sulk.

Gloating isn't necessary when winning and alibis and tantrums when losing take away from the general good feeling of the game. After the game, it's traditional to approach the net, shake hands, and for the winner to tell the loser, "nice game." After a game, sit down and analyze your mistakes. You'll be better prepared the next time.

SELF-CONTROL

Along with attitude, self-control is an attribute. Keep your mind on the game and keep fighting, whether you are winning or losing. Don't allow yourself to become distracted or annoyed. Losing your temper is an absolute sin. Everyone misses shots and everyone makes mistakes—including the best players in the world. Keep your cool at all times.

If an umpire and linesmen were assigned to your match, you and your opponent might feel that a few inaccurate decisions were made during the course of the match. Learn to accept all decisions in a sportsmanlike manner. The lineman is in a better position to make a judgment than you are.

STAY IN YOUR CLASS

Try to find opponents near your level of playing ability. A one-sided game isn't fun for you or for your opponent. If you overmatch yourself, you will try too hard. This will only result in errors, and frustration for both players.

However, if you have been practicing faithfully and feel that your game has improved, a game with a better player can be beneficial. You have already learned the proper attitude when playing with opponents who are below your class. You'll get the same courtesy when you are attempting to step up in class.

KEEP MOVING

It isn't good form to deliberately stall for a breather. You should be in ready stance as soon as possible after a point is scored. Stalling could also be detrimental to your game, since one of your objectives—and a frequently used strategy—is to wear down your opponent. The server has to be sure, before delivering, that the receiver is ready.

CALLING SCORES AND SERVES

If you are playing without the benefit of an umpire and linesmen, which will undoubtedly be the case in the beginning, the server has the responsibility to

Win or lose, your manner should reflect enjoyment. Accept your opponent's congratulations and respond with, "Nice game."

Jumping the net to congratulate an opponent is unnecessary and could be embarrassing and dangerous.

call the scores. It is the responsibility of the receiver to call close serves either "good" or "out." When in doubt, it is good manners to give your opponent the benefit of the call. If any question arises, replay the point.

RETRIEVING BALLS

Do nothing if your ball goes into another court where play is in progress. Even though you might not interfere with the action, your presence might be distracting. Wait until the action has stopped before retrieving your ball. Or, if more convenient, ask the other player to return the ball. The same is true when a ball from another court turns up on yours. Return it at the first break in your own play. You should return the ball with a soft toss rather than hitting it with your racket to the waiting player.

SACRIFICE

Unless you have hired a court for a specific period of time, remember that others are waiting to play, so vacate your court upon completion of your match. If the players waiting outnumber the courts available, it is good manners to suggest a doubles match.

ON THE SIDELINES

If you are watching a match or waiting for a court, don't be a nuisance. Uninvited umpiring and unasked-for advice are taboo. If a long waiting period causes you to "tighten," walk, jog, and dress warmly so that you don't cool off, but restrict your activities to where you won't be distracting to the players. If you are watching a match while waiting, it's permissible to applaud an exceptional shot, but don't go overboard. Audibly cheering for one player over the other is also frowned upon.

CLOTHING

Brightly colored, "busy" clothing and outlandish dress can be disconcerting to an opponent and are out of place on a tennis court. (See chapter 2 for proper and acceptable clothing for tennis play.)

One unwritten safety rule is worth mentioning here. Don't jump the net to congratulate your opponent. Simply walk to the net and shake hands. Jumping the net can result in severe injury, not to mention loss of dignity when your foot gets caught and you crash to the ground.

10 Strategy

Stamina and strength do not beat an opponent in tennis, strategy and psychology do. A part of strategy is taking advantage of what you know. With time, you will learn your weak points and strong points.

It is more important to attempt to learn the weak points and strong points of your opponents. The more you play with a person the more you will learn about him. If you are facing an opponent for the first time, use the warm-up period to acquaint yourself with his style of playing.

WHEN SERVING

When you are serving, you are in control of the ball. Learn to use this to your advantage. Vary the placement of your shots. Try to make your opponent move to meet the ball, thereby pulling him out of position. Later, try to throw him off balance by serving directly to him.

Serve to his forehand, then switch to his backhand, which, in the case of most beginners, is a weakness. The point is that it is good strategy to keep the receiver guessing about the placement of your shots.

You will soon be able to determine if your opponent prefers high or low bounces. If he is adept at returning a high-bounding ball, give him a low-bounding slice serve with as much spin as possible. If he seems to handle low balls well, give him a high-bounding serve. It is bad strategy, though, to serve all high-bounding or all low-bounding serves. Keep your opponent guessing by changing your tactics.

RETURN OF SERVICE

You know your opponent has the advantage when serving, but with proper strategy you might be able to force him to make errors. Play it cool. Do not attempt to win a point on your first return of service—just try to get the ball back and keep it in play.

If possible, return the ball to your opponent's weak side. This will put him on the defensive. Vary your return and you will be able to confuse your opponent.

Rush the net whenever possible, but stay in your back court when your opponent rushes in to follow his service. Keep your eyes on the ball and use your head. A deep lob will break his attack. A fast ball with plenty of topspin or a return aimed directly at his feet will force him to volley upward.

Make your opponent work hard to win his services. If you can tire him and out-psych him you will lessen his advantage over you.

RALLIES

Eventually you will learn when to rush to the net and when to stay back. Generally, if you are inside your base line you should follow your return, and when you are behind your base line you should stay back. Much depends, however, on whether your opponent is in or out of position. If he is *in* position, try to drive deep with a strong stroke and then follow it in to the net. If your opponent is *out* of position, drive deep and hard to a far corner, thus forcing him to return at a narrow angle. Hopefully, you will be ready and waiting to drop the ball in just over the net.

If your opponent finds you out of position, keep in mind that rushing the net is not a wise move because you are now on the defensive Wait for a more favorable opportunity to go in.

If you feel your judgment was wrong or you find yourself off balance, try to make your return as deep as possible. In other words, put the ball far back into your opponent's court to give yourself time to get back into position.

You will probably encounter some opponents who excel at the base line and are weak at the net. In such a case, it is good strategy to draw him away from the comfort of his favorite position. Lure him to the net with shots that must be played close to the net.

WINNING STRATEGY

In chapter 12 you will learn that the pros make a point of finding out all there is to know about an opponent. The more you learn about the strength and weaknesses of your opponent, the better able you will be to make full use of strategy. Out-psyching your opponent is an important feature of the modern tennis game.

Remember, it isn't possible to win a point with every stroke. Concentrate on keeping the ball in play until you find the right spot for your offensive attack.

If you have studied the weaknesses of your opponent, chances are he has also studied yours, so work on developing your weak strokes. Perhaps practice will not make your game perfect, but it will at least enable you to play a well-rounded game.

Learn to use the elements of surprise and deception. Vary your shots. If you keep your opponent guessing, you will force him to make errors. At the same time, disguise your shots by keeping your footwork and strokes in both forehand and backhand areas as alike as possible, with the variation coming at the moment the racket makes contact with the ball. If a certain movement or group of movements is always followed by a specific stroke, you will be telegraphing that shot and an alert opponent will always be ready to receive and counter it. Take chances now and then. Mix your shots and your timing. Even if you lose points in the process you are, at the same time, improving your attack.

Remember not to overattack a weakness, or you may be playing exactly the way your opponent is expecting you to. You *may* know his weaknesses, but he certainly does, and he has undoubtedly been practicing to overcome his handicap. If you do not get the upper hand with a confusion of shots, you will probably end up being the one who is confused.

Another important part of strategy is learning to control your emotions. If you become heated and angry, the tension will surely affect your game. If you feel tight, take a deep breath and deliberately slow yourself down. Playing loose is a definite advantage; a rattled player will only end up out-psyching himself. If you *look* cool, casual, and ready for anything, you could unnerve an attacking opponent and place him on the defensive.

A positive attitude is your best defensive weapon.

11
Keeping Score

OFFICIALS

Officials are used in important matches. An umpire, sitting in a high chair at one end of the net, keeps and calls out the score.

There is a lineman at each end of each sideline, each base line, each service line, and each center line—a total of fourteen people. A fifteenth person keeps his hand on the net near the post to be able to feel a let. Linesmen signal "good" or "out" to the umpire. A referee is present and can be appealed to if there is a question regarding the umpire's decision.

SCORING

Scoring appears to be complicated because it is based on tradition rather than employing practical math. The system, however, is quite simple, using only four units of scoring: point, game, set, and match, with the point being the smallest unit of scoring.

Game: If a player wins his first point, his score is 15; his score is 30 on winning his second point, and 40 on his third point. The fourth point wins the game.

If each player has scored three points (40–40) the score is called *deuce* and then the next point after deuce is called *advantage* or *ad.* If the player with the advantage scores the following point, he wins the game. If the other player scores the point, the score becomes deuce again. This continues until a player wins the two points following a score at deuce.

A zero score is called *love.* So when one player scores you will hear the server (or umpire) call the score "love–15" or "15–love." The server's score is always called first.

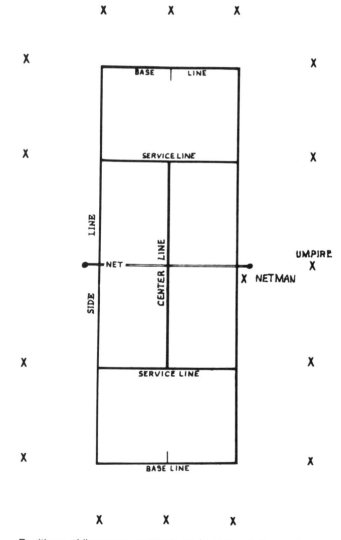

Positions of linesmen, netman, and umpire during an important match.

When the score is even (15–15 or 30–30) it is called *all* or *up*, so the server (or umpire) would call "15-all" or "30-all." As mentioned previously, a 40–40 tie would be called deuce.

In calling an advantage score, the server (or umpire) would call "server's advantage" or "ad in." When the receiver has the advantage the call made is "receiver's advantage" or "ad out." The serve, as you know by this time, is alternated on every game.

Set: The first player to win six games wins a set. However, if each player has five games, the score is called "games all" and the next game won is scored as an advantage game. If the player wins the next game he has won the set. If the opponent wins the next game, it's back to games all until a player wins two games more than his opponent.

A player can win by scores of 6–love, 6–1, 6–2, 6–3 or 6–4, but a 6–5 would not be a set because he has not won two games more than his opponent. In that case, play continues and might wind up with scores such as 7–5, 8–6, and so forth.

Match: The match is the best two out of three sets for women and best three out of five sets for men, except a two-out-of-three match is often used for men's competition in tournament play. Match scores are called with the match winner's score given first.

For example, if Arthur Ashe defeats Stan Smith 6–4 and 6–3 but also loses a set 6–2, the score would be given as 6–4, 6–3, 2–6, with Ashe's score for each set given first.

TIE BREAKING

Various systems of tie breakers are being tried with the hope that one system will eventually be adopted. While a 6–0, 6–1, 6–0 match might be played in forty-five minutes, other matches can last as long as several hours. This can be grueling for the players as well as the spectators.

Something must eventually be done to settle the question of a prolonged game. Increased television coverage also demands a more precise time schedule, so it is expected that one of the systems now being used on an experimental basis will eventually be used universally.

For the time being, after 5–5 or 6–6 a set might be decided by players taking turns serving until one player achieves one or two points. In other cases, a tie breaker is a nine-point game which means the player winning five points has the game.

In doubles, a nine-point system can be used, but a twelve-point tie breaker seems to be preferred so far. The team winning seven of the first twelve points wins. If neither team has scored seven points, the teams change ends and each player alternately serves to different sides.

So far the tie breakers are not clearly defined but hopefully a decision will be made in the near future.

12
A Look at the Pros

A pro has mastered the game of tennis but still must go several steps further. In addition to constant practice, a pro will learn all there is to know about an opponent—mannerisms, likes, dislikes, weaknesses. How strong is my opponent's backhand? Can my opponent return my best shot? Does my opponent excel at playing the back court or the net?

If the opponent is well studied in advance, he or she won't have a chance to play his or her favorite style of game. Every pro is a superb tactician. This highly mental approach to tennis is what distinguishes the professionals from the amateurs.

On the other hand, if both opponents are pros and if they have done their studies well, you will be treated to a great match incorporating stamina, skill, and perfection of the art.

Some players are better on certain surfaces—some excel indoors, some outdoors. Studying playing habits and preferences is an important tactic.

For example, if you were playing Evonne Goolagong you would learn that she is an expert at the backhand volley. She can topspin or slice it with equal ease. Evonne covers the court well and calculates her returns very carefully. She meets a ball well out in front, like Arthur Ashe. To outmaneuver this sensational little Australian, the opponent will have to know that Evonne has a weak second serve and that she'll make errors when under pressure. However, a game cannot be played with fingers crossed waiting for errors.

Arthur Ashe and Bob Lutz also excel with backhand volleys. Ashe, especially, has an effective backhand volley because he meets the ball way out in front of his body. He has unbelievable coordination of eye and hand. Ashe's only weakness seems to be his playing moods—he's either "on" or "off." If Arthur is "on" and using his backhand, he cannot be beaten. His calmness makes him a dangerous opponent. He serves with a mighty swing and excels on grass courts. He shouldn't be allowed to get into a comfortable groove—a wise opponent will change the pace often and vary the service.

An outstanding player, even under pressure, is Rod Laver—a left-hander. He knows he's great and his confidence shows. Laver is a tough competitor and is known to play a wide open, unpredictable game. He's the perfect example of a pro knowing the weaknesses of his opponents and applying the pressure where it hurts the most. Rod is particularly adept at return-of-service but has a weak smash. Due to back trouble, he's unable to stretch without caution. Back trouble or not, Rod is the only player to have won the grand slam twice and he won almost $300,000 in 1971. It's said that he excels indoors, but it is obvious that he excels anywhere with his sizzling forehands and backhands, sharp chip shots, and that wicked overspin.

Margaret Smith Court seems to be impossible to overpower because of her strength and speed. Her opponents can only attempt to keep the ball away from her. If Margaret gets an early lead—watch out. Her opponents will usually fold under the pressure. Margaret, the top money winner in women's tennis in 1973, has five doubles championships and is only two titles away from the record of seven presently

Evonne Goolagong   Arthur Ashe   Rod Laver

Ilie Nastase

Chris Evert

held by Helen (Wills) Roark. Margaret's opponents can relax now, as she will be retiring soon. She was, and is, a great champion.

Ilie Nastase, the "bad boy" of tennis (and often called Ilie "Nasty" by his opponents) is considered to be one of tennis's best players, along with Stan Smith, so he can't be all that bad. Smith, himself, suggests ignoring Ilie's court antics as it probably means Ilie is under pressure and is simply trying to relieve it by clowning around. At any rate, that certainly seems to work when Smith is facing Nastase.

In addition to his clowning, Ilie can swiftly return just about any stroke sent his way and runs to cover the entire court with the greatest of ease. He's a master at the drop shot. Tennis etiquette seems to have no meaning to Ilie, who has total disregard for everything and everyone—including the officials. In

1973 Ilie was fined over ten thousand dollars. He's moody and controversial but also shrewd and confident, and one of the best players in the world.

The opponents of Chris Evert marvel at her cool and poise under pressure, but she has been known to become frustrated when she wants to get the point over quickly, so an opponent must play with accuracy and patience. Chris has such an outward coolness and sophistication that she can easily out-psych her opponents. She doesn't take wild chances and knows exactly what she does well and then just does it well. Chris is one of the few players to effectively use a two-handed backhand, but then she's been swinging a racket since she was five years old. Her two-handed grip is an excellent example of practice makes perfect.

Jim Connors is a young rebel but not in the Ilie

Jim Connors

Ken Rosewall

Nastase sense. Jimmy believes in setting his own lifestyle and calling his own shots. He is the only major U.S. star who did not sign with World Championship Tennis for 1974, nor is he a member of the Association of Tennis Pros. In spite of his independence, he earned over $100,000 in 1973. Jimmy has been coached by both Pancho Gonzales and Pancho Segura and shows their influence in his play. He has great concentration, excels with ground strokes, and hits a blistering ball.

The 1974 singles titles at Wimbledon were won by Jimmy Connors (who beat out favorite Ken Rosewall) and Chris Evert.

Kerry Melville of Australia is new to the pro ranks and seems to have problems getting settled in her game, but once she is she gives her best for a good all-around game. She uses a lot of topspin on her

balls and she's lightning fast. Her opponents have to mix up their shots to confuse her but, with the progress she's been making, it's getting harder all the time to confuse her.

Ken Rosewall, another Australian, is a master at return-of-service, but, on the other hand, he has a semiweak serve. A hard return is apt to throw him off his game. His weak serve, however, seems to be helped by the slower synthetic surfaces and he excels indoors. Ken seems to have a knack for disguising almost all shots, especially his backhand volley.

The elegant and ever-smiling Vijay Amritraj is also a master at return-of-service. A few years ago Vijay was number ten in India. With his stunning victories, he's now on the heels of the top stars. He's tall, six-foot-three, and lean. His long reach and long legs enable him to cover the court well. He

79

shows remarkable poise and calmness. His happy mode of playing caused a sensation at the 1973 Wimbledon. Vijay seems to profit by his mistakes and he is expected to become one of the world's best.

Erik van Dillen excels at doubles play and plays especially well with partner Stan Smith. Their most outstanding (and historic) victory was their win against Romania in the 1972 Davis Cup championship. The pressures created by their opponent, Nastase, the belligerent crowds, and biased officials made the chances of a U.S. win almost impossible, but the combination of van Dillen and Smith triumphed over all obstacles. Van Dillen was also a participant with Smith in the longest doubles match in Davis Cup history—a six hours and thirty minutes five-set match with a grueling 37–39 second set lasting three hours and forty-five minutes. Needless to say, Eric's net play was absolutely brilliant.

What can be said about Stan Smith except that he is the world's *best*. Stan shares top honors with Nastase, but on the court he shares with no one. The six-foot-four Smith blankets the court with seemingly endless long arms and legs that appear to be everywhere. He employs complete concentration and has powerful serves, especially a big first serve. His shots and volleys are magnificent. Stan's height also helps him with his brilliant overhead shots. Stan can play anywhere, any surface, any way, and anyone. A search for weaknesses revealed none. No wonder he was the top World Championship money winner in 1973.

New to the scene is Brian Gottfried of Florida, who held his own as a rookie against the likes of Rod Laver and Stan Smith. He destroyed Arthur Ashe in the 1973 Alan King Classic in Las Vegas and captivated the crowd with his play, his Fu Manchu moustache and long face complete with twisted nose. He swings loose and easy and plays a good all-around game with no apparent weaknesses, except for a fixed style and a tendency to brood if he is beaten by a lesser player. He believes in hard work and a lot of practice, and was once coached by Jim Evert, father and coach of Chris and Jeanne. Brian shows solid ground strokes. He has a solid smash similar to that of Stan Smith and excels at volleys.

Billie Jean King needs no introduction to tennis

In his pre-mustache days, Stan Smith (left) and partner Bob Lutz (right) won the NCAA doubles championship for Southern California in 1967 and 1968.

Stan Smith

Brian Gottfried

Billie Jean King

Marita Redondo

fans. She is simply the best woman tennis player in the world and the first woman to go over $100,000 in winnings—and this does *not* include her price money for trouncing Bobby Riggs in the highly touted "Tennis Match of the Century" at the Houston Astrodome on Sept. 20, 1973. Billie Jean is president of the newly formed Women's Tennis Association and started Tennis America, Inc., a teaching organization with various tennis camp locations. She was one of the first player-coaches signed for World Team Tennis. She led the battle to gain recognition for women players and deserves full credit for creating a boom in women's tennis. While Billie Jean was doing all this, she continued to win her fair share on the battlefields of the tennis courts. She is truly a remarkable woman as well as an outstanding player.

A rookie to watch is Marita Redondo, the teen sensation from California. She's already beaten such established pros as Evonne Goolagong and has given Chris Evert a battle or two. Another teen on the scene is Chris's sister, Jeanne Evert. She might be at a disadvantage because of her height, a tiny

Pancho Gonzales

Cliff Richey

five-foot-one, but she's barely sixteen years old and might sprout a few more inches. In addition, Jeanne has been coached by Papa Evert, who has a good coaching record going for him. Robin Tenney is also a young newcomer. She's from California, sixteen years old, and she's anxious to show the world what she can do.

Roscoe Tanner, former college teammate of Brian Gottfried, has a fearful serve and has beaten Nastase. He'll be one to watch in the future, along with the long-haired, shy, Swedish sensation, Bjorn Borg, who has become the idol of the young set.

The pro ranks are bulging with fine players so it is impossible to mention every player in this brief chapter. If your favorite has been omitted, it's due to lack of space rather than to lack of talent.

Brief mention should be made of great old-timers such as Pancho Segura and Pancho Gonzales. Gonzales is nearing fifty but he is still a master and has often been called the greatest player in the history of the sport. John Newcombe is another who has been on the scene for a long time. Newcombe is always fit and still a threat—especially in indoor play.

High in the women's circuit are Francoise Durr of France, and Americans Rosemary Casals, Valerie Ziegenfuss, Janet Newbury, Patti Hogan, Nancy Gunter, and Julie Heldman, who beat Billie Jean in a controversial upset blamed on heat and the illness of Queen King. Controversial or not, Julie has proved herself to be an outstanding competitor.

Virginia Wade of England is another tough contender and is adept at rushing the net to overcome drop shots. Her outstanding frontal attack makes her excel at doubles.

In the men's circuit, we have Cliff Drysdale, who excells indoors; Dick Stockton, who has upset Stan Smith; the Soviet Union's powerful Alex Metreveli; Cliff Richey; and Tom Okker, who plays a well-rounded game. Okker, "The Flying Dutchman," is a drop-shot master and has beaten top pros such as Newcombe.

More top players are: Roger Taylor, a left-hander from England; colorful Nikki Pilic, a drop-shot expert whose only apparent problem is a weak smash; Roy Emerson; and Harold Solomon, a spunky young man who sports a two-handed backhand.

Tom Gorman is consistently good and has an outstanding smash. Tom relies on mental attitude, which is good self-training. He helps himself along by leaving notes for himself in his racket cover and

Manuel Orantes

reads them between sets. "Move" and "be consistent," Tom might memo himself.

Wimbledon champion Jan Kodes of Czechoslovakia is another who is moving swiftly upward to stardom.

Watch for Manuel Orantes, a flashy, brilliant left-hander from Spain. Clay court champion in 1973, he is barking at the heels of the top-seeded players. Also keep an eye on Adriano Panatta, who is number one in Italy, Raul Ramirez of Mexico, and Ion Tiriac of Romania.

Stars of the future could be Onny Parun, Karl Meiler, Betty Stove, John Bartlett, Helga Masmastoff, Clark Graebner, Marty Riesen, Pam Teeguarden, Linda Tuero, Paul Gerken, and Martina Navratilovna.

The list is endless. To add your name to this distinguished list, learn your lessons well.

13 Wrap-Up

It's important to start correctly, or your later development will be restricted. Practice, play, practice, learn, practice, watch, practice, and above all, practice. Learn to master sound strokes with pace and accuracy before attempting to learn new approaches and variations.

Play for each point *one at a time*. Remember, your forehand is your main stroke, so learn it well and it will turn out to be your most trusted shot.

Don't play your first match until you feel you are ready for it, otherwise you might become discouraged. If you have mastered your forehand, your backhand is reasonably strong, and you feel that you can lob and volley with some chance of success, then, by all means, try to win your first match.

Win or lose, practice again as soon as possible —immediately after the match if you can. If some of your strokes did not feel sound, practice those. Practice is the best cure for overcoming a weakness. If your weakness continues to haunt you, go to the library and read every tennis book you can find. Chances are someone else had the same problem, found a cure, and wrote about it.

Remember, speed is not as important as reaction, timing, court position, and the ability to anticipate your opponents' shots, but it will come in time.

Tennis is challenging and quite complicated in the beginning, so be patient. If you expect to walk out on the court and start hitting the ball over the net —forget it. It's a simple game but it takes time and practice to master. Keep a positive mental attitude. Don't be a quitter.

Even the pros feel some degree of tension, so don't be embarrassed if you feel nervous. Utilize your warm-up period to settle yourself as much as possible.

The more you play, the more you'll learn about the game. If your game doesn't improve as rapidly as you want it to, start again with the basics. With practice you will find the cause of your weakness, then you can concentrate on overcoming it.

Tennis is a game for all ages, seven to seventy, and for all skill levels. Even the novice can participate actively and enjoy hours of exhilarating recreation in an animated and friendly atmosphere. With the recent proliferation of indoor courts, tennis has happily become a year-round activity, allowing more players than ever to get in the swing and meet new challenges and friends on the courts. Won't you pick up your racket and join them?

The tennis court—where friendly games end and friendships begin.

14 Official Rules *

EXPLANATORY NOTE

The appended Code of Rules is the official code of the International Lawn Tennis Federation, of which the United States Lawn Tennis Association is a member.

THE SINGLES GAME

RULE 1

Dimensions and Equipment

The court shall be a rectangle, 78 feet long and 27 feet wide. It shall be divided across the middle by a net, suspended from a cord or metal cable of a maximum diameter of ⅓ of an inch, the ends of which shall be attached to, or pass over, the tops of two posts, 3 feet 6 inches high, the center of which shall be 3 feet outside the court on each side. The height of the net shall be 3 feet at the center, where it shall be held down taut by a strap not more than 2 inches wide. There shall be a band covering the cord or metal cable and the top of the net not less than 2 inches nor more than 2½ inches in depth on each side. The lines bounding the ends and sides of the court shall respectively be called the base lines and the sidelines. On each side of the net, at a distance of 21 feet from it and parallel with it, shall be drawn the service lines. The space on each side of the net between the service line and the sidelines shall be divided into two equal parts called the service courts by the center service line, which must be 2 inches in width, drawn halfway between, and parallel with, the sidelines. Each base line shall be bisected by an imaginary continuation of the center service line to a line 4 inches in length and 2 inches in width called the center mark drawn inside the court, at right angles to and in contact with such base lines. All other lines shall not be less than 1 inch nor more than 2 inches in width, except the base line, which may be 4 inches in width, and all measurements shall be made to the outside of the lines.

Note—In the case of the International Lawn Tennis Championship (Davis Cup) or other official championships of the International Federation, there shall be a space behind each base line of not less than 21 feet and at the sides of not less than 12 feet.

* Excerpted and edited from *Rules of Lawn Tennis* provided by the United States Lawn Tennis Association.

RULE 2

Permanent Fixtures

The permanent fixtures of the court shall include not only the net, posts, cord or metal cable, strap and band, but also, where there are any such, the back and side stops, the stands, fixed or movable seats and chairs around the court, and their occupants, all other fixtures around and above the court, and the umpire, net-cord judge, foot-fault judge, linesmen, and ball boys when in their respective places.

RULE 3

Ball—Size, Weight, and Bound

The ball shall have a uniform outer surface and may be white or yellow in color. If there are any seams they shall be stitchless. The ball shall be more than 2½ inches and less than 2⅝ inches in diameter, and more than 2 ounces and less than $2^1/_{16}$ ounces in weight. The ball shall have a bound of more than 53 inches and less than 58 inches when dropped 100 inches upon a concrete base. The ball shall have a forward deformation of more than .230 of an inch and less than .290 of an inch and a return reformation of more than .355 of an inch and less than .425 of an inch at 18-lb. load. The two deformation figures shall be the average of three individual readings along three axes of the ball and no two individual readings shall differ by more than .030 of an inch in each case. All tests for bound, size and deformation shall be made in accordance with regulations.

Note—At the Annual General Meeting of the I.L.T.F. held on July 12, 1967, it was agreed that for the time being nonpressurized balls and low-pressure balls may not be used in the International Lawn Tennis Championship (Davis Cup), unless mutually agreed by the two nations taking part in any particular event.

RULE 4

Server and Receiver

The players shall stand on opposite sides of the net; the player who first delivers the ball shall be called the server, and the other the receiver.

RULE 5

Choice of Sides and Service

The choice of sides and the right to be server or receiver in the first game shall be decided by toss. The player winning the toss may choose, or require his opponent to choose:
  (a) The right to be server or receiver, in which case the other player shall choose the side; or
  (b) The side, in which case the other player shall choose the right to be server or receiver.

RULE 6

Delivery of Service

The service shall be delivered in the following manner: Immediately before commencing to serve, the server shall stand with both feet at rest behind (i.e. farther from the net than) the base line, and within the imaginary continuations of the center mark and sideline. The server shall then project the ball by hand into the air in any direction and before it hits the ground strike it with his racket, and the delivery shall be deemed to have been completed at the moment of the impact of the racket and the ball. A player with the use of only one arm may utilize his racket for the projection.

RULE 7

Foot Fault

The server shall throughout the delivery of the service:
  (a) Not change his position by walking or running.
  (b) Not touch, with either foot, any area other than that behind the base line within the imaginary extension of the center mark and sideline.

RULE 8

From Alternate Courts

  (a) In delivering the service, the server shall stand alternately behind the right and left courts, beginning from the right in every game. If service from a wrong half of the court occurs and is undetected, all play resulting from such wrong service or services shall stand, but the

inaccuracy of the station shall be corrected immediately when it is discovered.
  (b) The ball served shall pass over the net and hit the ground within the service court which is diagonally opposite, or upon any line bounding such court, before the receiver returns it.

RULE 9

Faults

The service is a fault:
  (a) If the server commits any breach of Rules 6, 7, or 8;
  (b) If he misses the ball in attempting to strike it;
  (c) If the ball served touches a permanent fixture (other than the net, strap, or band) before it hits the ground.

RULE 10

Service After a Fault

After a fault (if it be the first fault) the server shall serve again from behind the same half of the court from which he served that fault, unless the service was from the wrong half, when, in accordance with Rule 8, the server shall be entitled to one service only from behind the other half. A fault may not be claimed after the next service has been delivered.

RULE 11

Receiver Must Be Ready

The server shall not serve until the receiver is ready. If the latter attempts to return the service, he shall be deemed ready. If, however, the receiver signifies that he is not ready, he may not claim a fault because the ball does not hit the ground within the limits fixed for the service.

RULE 12

A Let

In all cases where a let has to be called under the rules, or to provide for an interruption to play, it shall have the following interpretations:
  (a) When called solely in respect of a service, that one service only shall be replayed.
  (b) When called under any other circumstance, the point shall be replayed.

RULE 13

Service Is a Let
The service is a let:
- (a) If the ball served touches the net, strap, or band, and is otherwise good, or, after touching the net, strap or band, touches the receiver or anything which he wears or carries before hitting the ground.
- (b) If a service or a fault is delivered when the receiver is not ready (see Rule 11).

RULE 14

When Receiver Becomes Server
At the end of the first game the receiver shall become the server, and the server receiver; and so on alternately in all the subsequent games of a match. If a player serves out of turn, the player who ought to have served shall serve as soon as the mistake is discovered, but all points scored before such discovery shall be reckoned. If a game shall have been completed before such discovery, the order of service remains as altered. A fault served before such discovery shall not be reckoned.

RULE 15

Ball in Play Till Point Decided
A ball is in play from the moment at which it is delivered in service. Unless a fault or a let is called, it remains in play until the point is decided.

RULE 16

Server Wins Point
The server wins the point:
- (a) If the ball served, not being a let under Rule 13, touches the receiver or anything which he wears or carries, before it hits the ground;
- (b) If the receiver otherwise loses the point as provided by Rule 18.

RULE 17

Receiver Wins Point
The receiver wins the point:
- (a) If the server serves two consecutive faults;
- (b) If the server otherwise loses the point as provided by Rule 18.

RULE 18

Player Loses Point
A player loses the point if:
- (a) He fails, before the ball in play has hit the ground twice consecutively, to return it directly over the net (except as provided in Rule 22 (a) or (c)); or
- (b) He returns the ball in play so that it hits the ground, a permanent fixture, or other object, outside any of the lines which bound his opponent's court (except as provided in Rule 22 (a) and (c)); or
- (c) He volleys the ball and fails to make a good return even when standing outside the court; or
- (d) He touches or strikes the ball in play with his racket more than once in making a stroke; or
- (e) He or his racket (in his hand or otherwise) or anything which he wears or carries touches the net, posts, cord or metal cable, strap or band, or the ground within his opponent's court at any time while the ball is in play; or
- (f) He volleys the ball before it has passed the net; or
- (g) The ball in play touches him or anything that he wears or carries, except his racket in his hand or hands; or
- (h) He throws his racket at and hits the ball.

RULE 19

Player Hinders Opponent
If a player commits any act either deliberate or involuntary which, in the opinion of the umpire, hinders his opponent in making a stroke, the umpire shall in the first case award the point to the opponent, and in the second case order the point to be replayed.

RULE 20

Ball Falling on Line—Good
A ball falling on a line is regarded as falling in the court bounded by that line.

RULE 21

Ball Touching Permanent Fixture
If the ball in play touches a permanent fixture (other than the net, posts, cord or metal cable, strap

or band) after it has hit the ground, the player who struck it wins the point; if before it hits the ground his opponent wins the point.

RULE 22

Good Return

It is a good return:
(a) If the ball touches the net, posts, cord or metal cable, strap or band, provided that it passes over any of them and hits the ground within the court; or
(b) If the ball, served or returned, hits the ground within the proper court and rebounds or is blown back over the net, and the player whose turn it is to strike reaches over the net and plays the ball, provided that neither he nor any part of his clothes or racket touch the net, posts, cord or metal cable, strap or band or the ground within his opponent's court, and that the stroke be otherwise good; or
(c) If the ball is returned outside the post, either above or below the level of the top of the net, even though it touches the post, provided that it hits the ground within the proper court; or
(d) If a player's racket passes over the net after he has returned the ball, provided the ball passes the net before being played and is properly returned; or
(e) If a player succeeded in returning the ball, served or in play, which strikes a ball lying in the court.

RULE 23

Interference

In case a player is hindered in making a stroke by anything not within his control except a permanent fixture of the court, or except as provided for in Rule 19, the point shall be replayed.

RULE 24

The Game

If a player wins his first point, the score is called *15* for that player; on winning his second point, the score is called *30* for that player; on winning his third point, the score is called *40* for that player, and the fourth point won by a player is scored *game* for that player except as below:
If both players have won three points, the score is

called *deuce*; and the next point won by a player is called *advantage* for that player. If the same player wins the next point, he wins the game; if the other player wins the next point the score is again called *deuce*; and so on until a player wins the two points immediately following the score at deuce, when the game is scored for that player.

RULE 25

The Set

A player (or players) who first wins six games wins a set; except that he must win by a margin of two games over his opponent and where necessary a set shall be extended until this margin be achieved.

RULE 26

When Players Change Sides

The players shall change sides at the end of the first, third, and every subsequent alternate game of each set, and at the end of each set unless the total number of games in such set is even, in which case the change is not made until the end of the first game of the next set.

RULE 27

Maximum Number of Sets

The maximum number of sets in a match shall be five, or, where women take part, three.

RULE 28

Rules Apply to Both Sexes

Except where otherwise stated, every reference in these rules to the masculine includes the feminine gender.

RULE 29

Decisions of Umpire and Referee

In matches where an umpire is appointed, his decision shall be final; but where a referee is appointed, an appeal shall lie to him from the decision of an umpire on a question of law, and in all such cases the decision of the referee shall be final, except that in Davis Cup and Federation Cup matches the decision of a lineman can be changed by the referee, or by the umpire with the consent of the referee.

The referee, in his discretion, may at any time postpone a match on account of darkness, or the condition of the ground, or the weather. In any case of postponement the previous score and previous occupancy of courts shall hold good, unless the referee and the players unanimously agree otherwise.

RULE 30

Play shall be continuous from the first service till the match is concluded; provided that after the third set or when women take part, the second set, either player is entitled to a rest, which shall not exceed ten minutes, or in countries situated between latitude 15 degrees north and latitude 15 degrees south, 45 minutes, and provided further that when necessitated by circumstances not within the control of the players, the umpire may suspend play for such a period as he may consider necessary. If play is suspended and is not resumed until a later day, the rest may be taken only after the third set (or when women take part the second set) of play on such later day, completion of an unfinished set being counted as one set. These provisions shall be strictly construed, and play shall never be suspended, delayed, or interfered with for the purpose of enabling a player to recover his strength or his wind, or to receive instruction or advice. The umpire shall be the sole judge of such suspension, delay, or interference, and after giving due warning he may disqualify the offender.

THE DOUBLES GAME

RULE 31

The above rules shall apply to the doubles game except as below.

RULE 32

Dimension of Court

For the doubles game, the court shall be 36 feet in width, i.e., 4½ feet wider on each side than the court for the singles game, and those portions of the singles sidelines which lie between the two service lines shall be called the service sidelines. In other respects, the court shall be similar to that described in Rule 1, but the portions of the singles sidelines between the base line and service line on each side of the net may be omitted if desired.

RULE 33

Order of Service

The order of serving shall be decided at the beginning of each set as follows:

The pair who have to serve in the first game of each set shall decide which partner shall do so and the opposing pair shall decide similarly for the second game. The partner of the player who served in the first game shall serve in the third; the partner of the player who served in the second game shall serve in the fourth, and so on in the same order in all the subsequent games of a set.

RULE 34

Order of Receiving

The order of receiving the service shall be decided at the beginning of each set as follows:

The pair who have to receive the service in the first game shall decide which partner shall receive the first service, and that partner shall continue to receive the first service in every odd game throughout that set. The opposing pair shall likewise decide which partner shall receive the first service in the second game and that partner shall continue to receive the first service in every even game throughout that set. Partners shall receive the service alternately throughout each game.

RULE 35

Service Out of Turn

If a partner serves out of his turn, the partner who ought to have served shall serve as soon as the mistake is discovered, but all points scored, and any faults served before such discovery, shall be reckoned. If a game shall have been completed before such discovery, the order of service remains as altered.

RULE 36

Error in Order of Receiving

If during a game the order of receiving the service is changed by the receivers it shall remain as altered until the end of the game in which the mistake is discovered, but the partners shall resume their original order of receiving in the next game of that set in which they are receivers of the service.

RULE 37

Ball Touching Server's Partner Is Fault

The service is a fault as provided for by Rule 9, or if the ball served touches the server's partner or anything he wears or carries; but if the ball served touches the partner of the receiver or anything which he wears or carries, not being a let under Rule 13 (a), before it hits the ground, the server wins the point.

RULE 38

Ball Struck Alternately

The ball shall be struck alternately by one or other player of the opposing pairs, and if a player touches the ball in play with his racket in contravention of this rule, his opponents win the point.

Glossary

Ace: A service so well placed that it cannot be returned by an opponent.

Ad or Advantage: The point following a score of deuce (after the players have each won three points in the same game). The next point is called *ad* or *advantage* if the server has won the point, and *ad-out* or *advantage-out* if the receiver has won the point.

All: A tie or equal score.

Alley: Part of the doubles court consisting of the area of the court bounded by the singles sideline and the doubles sideline (used only in doubles after service has been put into play).

American Twist: A type of service in which the racket imparts topspin as well as sidespin to the ball, creating a high bounce.

Angle Game: A style of play in which the angles of the court are used in an attempt to volley strokes angled past an opponent.

Angled Volley: A volley hit diagonally across the court almost parallel to the net.

Approach Shot: A shot hit deep into the opponent's court, allowing the hitter to move toward the net.

Back Court: Area between service line and base line.

Backhand: A stroke made with the playing arm and racket across the body. The stroke is played on the left side of a right-handed player or on the right side of a left-handed player.

Backroom: Space between the base line and the court's backstop or fence.

Backspin: Reverse or backward rotation of the ball while in flight. Caused by a chop stroke.

Backswing: The initial wind-up of a stroke in a backward direction before the racket makes contact with the ball.

Base Line: Rear boundary line at either end of the court.

Block: The return of a ball by holding the racket stiffly in front of the body; backswing and follow-through are not used.

Break: When you win the other player's serve.

Bullet: A hard-hit ball.

Cannonball: A hard-hit, fast service.

Center Mark: A four-inch mark drawn inside the base line that bisects it and defines the limited area from which to serve.

Center Service Line: The line separating right and left service courts, also called half-court line.

Chip: A short chop which is used either to return service or as an approach shot.

Chop: An undercut slicing stroke hit in front of the body with very little wind-up or follow-through creating a sharp backspin or underspin.

Continental Grip: Refers to a forehand grip, with the hand turned well over on the top of the racket.

Crosscourt: A ball which is hit from one side of the court to the diagonally opposite side.

Davis Cup: Donated by Dwight Davis as a symbol of international tennis supremacy.

Deuce: A tie score; the score when *each* player has three points, four points, five points, and so forth.

Die: A ball that barely bounces.

93

Dink: A soft shot without spin which drops just as it comes over the net so an opponent cannot reach it. A dink is used to force a net player into error, or if he is able to reach the ball, to make him hit high.

Double Fault: Two consecutive errors in serving which result in loss of point.

Drive: A hard-hit forehand or backhand ground stroke which lands deep in the opponent's back court.

Drive Volley: A volley in which a ground stroke wind-up is taken, either forehand or backhand.

Drop Shot: A ground stroke hit softly but with so much underspin that it passes easily over the net, then drops with little or no bounce (dies).

Drop Volley: A volley hit easily and just over the net with so much underspin that it bounces like a drop shot.

Eastern Grip: Racket head is perpendicular to the ground and player "shakes hands" with the racket; hand is rotated for a backhand grip.

Error: Failure to make a legal return because of a mistake, or any ball that hits the net or the area outside the court boundaries. The player who commits the error loses the point.

Doubles: Competition consisting of two teams, two players each.

Face: Strings (hitting surface) within the head of the racket; *closed face:* face slanted forward, toward ground; *flat face:* face vertical to ground; *open face:* face tilting backward and pointed diagonally upward.

Fault: Improper serve or an error on first service. The player does not lose the point and is allowed another service without penalty. The ball must be served into the proper service court.

Fifteen: The first point that a player wins in a game.

Flat Serve: A service hit hard with little or no spin.

Flat Shot: A ground stroke without spin.

Follow-through: The motion of arm and racket after the ball has been hit.

Foot Fault: Illegal serve caused by illegal motions by server, such as illegal position, movement of feet before or during service, stepping on base line or into court.

Forced Error: Also called *forcing shot.* An error made by a player because of a good shot on the part of his opponent, who has kept the other player on the defense and out of position.

Forcing Shot: A shot which produces either an outright error or a weak return (see **Forced Error**).

Forecourt: Area between net and service line.

Forehand: A ball hit from the right side of a right-handed player and left side of a left-handed player.

Forty: Third point a player wins.

Game Score: Rather than 1, 2, 3, and 4, points are 15, 30, 40, and game. A game must be won by at least two points. If each player has three points (or 40) the score is deuce rather than 40–40 or 40–all.

Simplified:

points	score
0	Love
1	15
2	30
3	40
4	Game

Grand Slam: Winning, in one season, the U.S., Australian, French, and British national championships.

Grip: Racket handle; also manner in which racket is held.

Ground Stroke: A stroke hit after the ball has bounced. Opposite of volley.

Hack: Clumsy service.

Half-volley: A defensive shortened stroke hit immediately after the ball has bounded (usually because the player is not in a volleying position).

Hitting Deep: Hitting to an area on or within two or three feet of the base line.

Hitting Shot: Hitting into an area in the vicinity of the service line.

Kill Shot: Ball smashed out of reach of opponent.

Let: A ball touching the net on the serve but landing in the proper area; the point is replayed. Also, a let can refer to any stroke that must be replayed.

Lob: A ball hit in a high arc over the head of an opponent standing at the net.

Love: Zero or no points in scoring.

Match: Competition consisting of predetermined number of sets or games.

Match Point: Point needed to win match.

Mid-court: Central area in front of and behind the service line.

Net Ball: Any ball that hits the net other than on service. If the ball lands within the court boundaries, whether or not it touches the net, it is good and is in play.

Net Man: A player whose position is inside the service line near the net.

Odd Court: Left service court.

Offensive Volley: High volley made from net level.

Set Score: When a player wins at least six games and two more than his opponent.

Set Point: Point needed to win set.

Set-Up: An easy shot, usually a short, high ball.

Sideline: Side boundary of playing courts.

Singles: One player competing with another single opponent.

Slice Shot: Type of serve in which the racket comes across the ball sideways and forward at the same time, resulting in a sidespin.

Smash: Same as overhead shot.

Spin: A method of hitting which produces a rotation of ball in flight caused by a rolling of the ball either sideways (sidespin), forward (overspin or topspin), or backward (underspin).

Switch: Exchange of players' court positions to cover vacated area.

Thirty: The second point a player gets.

Throat: Where head of racket meets the handle.

Topspin: A forward rotation of the ball after it has been hit.

Overhead: A stroke hit directly over the head usually with the arm fully extended.

Passing Shot: A ball out of reach of opponent playing near net, hit down either side or across court.

Placement: A shot that cannot be touched or returned by opponent.

Poacher: Net man in doubles who invades his partner's area of the court in order to put away a volley.

Point: Smallest unit of score.

Rally: Hitting the ball back and forth across the net after the ball has bounced for a prolonged length of time.

Receiver: The person receiving the serve.

Scissors: Cross-over tactic in doubles; net man and the man in back court cross over to change positions.

Seeding: Separation of top-ranked players so the number-one player will get lesser opponents in the earlier rounds and meet the strongest opponents in the later rounds.

Server: The person serving the ball, thereby putting it into play.

Service Break: Winning a game your opponent has served; also called *broken service*.

95

Service Court: Area bounded by the net and service lines into which serves must land for singles or doubles play.

Service Line: Back boundry of service courts.

Toss: Also called *spinning*. Method of determining which player or team serves first and which side of the court the player or team will play to start. A coin can be tossed or the racket can be used. The tip of the racket is placed on the ground, spun, and allowed to fall, with the players calling "rough" or "smooth" or "top" or "bottom," referring to the trimming at the top of the racket face.

Touch Shot: Any shot that is produced by a delicate movement of the racket such as a drop shot, a lob volley, or an extremely angled shot.

Undercut: Hitting the ball on the bottom, creating a reverse spin.

Up: Equal score; same as *all*.

Volley: A ball that is hit in midair before it bounces.